MANIFESTING A
RICH
REALITY

LIFE PRINCIPLES TO MAKE YOUR
DREAMS BECOME YOUR REALITY

AMIR SHAHEED

Copyright © 2022 by Amir Shaheed

All rights reserved. No part of this book may be reproduced, stored, or transmitted by any means - whether auditory, graphic, mechanical, or electronic - without written permission of both publisher and author, except in the case of brief excerpts used in critical articles and certain other noncommercial uses permitted by copyright law. Unauthorized reproduction of any part of this work is illegal and is punishable by law.

ISBN 979-8-218-04667-5

Printed and bound in the United States of America

Book Designed by Brand It Beautifully™
www.branditbeautifully.com
allison@imallisondenise.com

DEDICATION

To every rich mind...which should be everyone.

CONTENTS

Acknowledgements. vi

Introduction vii

PART ONE

LOSING YOUR RICH REALITY

Chapter One: Disruptive Perspective 3

Chapter Two: Limits on a Rich Mind 11

Chapter Three: Three Sides to Every Story. . .19

Chapter Four: Self Sabotaging the Rich Mind. . 27

PART TWO

FINDING YOUR RICH REALITY

Chapter Five: The Awakening. 37

Chapter Six: The Pathway 43

Conclusion 57

About The Author 59

ACKNOWLEDGEMENTS

I WOULD LIKE to thank my Rich Reality tribe. All of you that continue to push me, guide me, support me, and encourage me to be my rich self.

INTRODUCTION

THE RICH REALITY

A RICH REALITY is the birthright of everyone. It's that place of bliss where there's no worries in the world: you're zoned in on passion, zoned in on things you love, and zoned in on what makes you tick. What's beautiful about it is that it can look however you want it to look. It could be loving the job you do, working out and living a long and healthy life, or having the ability to hang out with family whenever you feel like it. It could be finding joy in the smallest of things. It's really up to you. It's your individual perspective on what makes you happy and filled with joy. When we're born, we all enter the world with this innate perspective of happy possibilities. We're all born with a rich mindset. The challenge comes when that rich mindset is thwarted, undeveloped, or dulled.

You see, the problem is that, throughout time, life experiences can cause us to lose that rich reality through our programming and through other people's projected desires of what we should be doing with our lives. But I have good news! There is a way to get back to that place of bliss – there is a way to manifest the rich reality lying dormant inside of you. It starts with reactivating that rich mindset with which we are all innately born. I'm going to give you a guide on how your dreams can become your rich reality. However this is not just a guide, but also life principles you will be able to apply to your mind system. Tools for your everyday use.

Most people think you need money to live a rich reality, but this couldn't be further from the truth. A rich reality is NOT and will NEVER be based on material wealth, but is based on intangible ideas, mindsets, and energy. I got caught up in the rat race once before believing that this was true. I can remember my high school years, when they had these categories like Best Dressed or Most Likely to Succeed. These were ideas instilled in us by our mentors that, in retrospect, could be deemed as judgmental or detrimental to the self-esteem of someone that may not have even paid rent before! It certainly impacted how I viewed myself in comparison. Fortunately it didn't stop me making my dreams a rich reality, but it certainly acted as an obstacle along the way. It put me in subconscious competition with my peers when the only person I should have been in competition with was myself and my own mind. It had me basing my reality off of someone else's perception and definition of success.

Fresh out of high school, instead of exploring ways to make my dreams my rich reality, I chose from the program that was handed to me. I felt like I was expected to make fast decisions on what I was going to do in life and who I was going to become. So, I did. I chose the military and law enforcement. Now looking back, I'm unsure if I chose this because I was settling for something or because it was my pathway to my rich reality. Was this me dreaming big or me settling for a career because I was in this subconscious rat race, where I felt the need to hurry up and succeed before I was deemed a failure by society? So when did I lose touch with my rich reality? It was long before I graced the halls of my high school. It all started back when I was three years old – what I like to call the beginning of my comprehension.

PART ONE

LOSING YOUR RICH REALITY

CHAPTER ONE

DISRUPTIVE PERSPECTIVE

UNLIMITED PROSPERITY. THOSE were the words I got tattooed on my forearm at the age of 16. Growing up, I often felt people put limitations on my abilities – or just didn't really get them. From that was born an unshakeable desire to reassure myself that there were no limits to prosperity. Maybe it was the conformist views people had instilled in me along my journey, or maybe it was my reluctance to take the driver's seat in my own life and mind. Either way, coming into adulthood is when I finally had a chance to look back and evaluate. Have you ever watched a movie as a kid and then watched the very same movie as an adult? I do this all time. Well, the best way I can describe what a mental perspective shift looks like is to share with you one of my favorite childhood movies – Richie Rich. As a kid, Richie's idea of wealth was material possessions. To him that seemed like a rich reality. However, by the end of the movie they had a perspective shift and began to see that their true rich reality was family, with their most prized possessions being fond memories of family moments. Shifting perspectives in life can be a lot like this movie. A lot like what you thought of a movie as a child versus what you think of that same movie now. You remember what the movie was about scene by scene, but your perspective has changed since you last saw that movie. What this means is that even though you still have that childhood memory, you no longer have that same childhood perspective. As the saying goes, "when I was a child I spoke as a child, but now that I am older…" Well, you get the idea.

Remember in grade school, when you were overcome with urgency about something you just had to whisper to your friend a couple seats over, how you just had to tell them now? I had many a moment like this and, well, while I thought of it as a super important moment to socialize, my teacher thought it was disruptive. Can you say, 'singled out and separated from your classmates?'

Yep! That was me, as far back as first grade. As an adult, I'm still social and still have moments when something needs to be said right now! The difference? As adults, we don't usually find someone whispering to someone else while we're speaking disruptive. Why? It's all about perspective! How you see things – your perspective – makes all the difference.

As a 7-year-old who loved to talk, I recall my teachers calling my mother repeatedly about me being disruptive (AKA whispering to his fellow classmates). Upon reflection, I sometimes wish the older me was there to tell the younger me, "I see something great in you. You love speaking, so why not put it to good use? You should nominate yourself for class president!" How pivotal that would have been for my rich mind journey. It could have taught me early on the importance of seeing my character traits as a light within me vs. seeing them as flaws. Instead, I was subjected to shame.

Discipline in the first grade looked like my teacher placing a sticky note on my back with a label that read: MOST DISRUPTIVE KID IN CLASS. I felt it was a bit excessive, being labeled by the teacher and then having to walk around school with all the other kids and teachers labeling you, too. I call those days "walk of shame days." I remember them well and I highly disliked being unobjectively judged by others based on someone else's perspective of me.

You see, we create biases with an unobjective mindset, forgetting that there are three sides to every story. Yes: three, not two. The subjective view, which is more opinion-based vs. fact-based. The objective view, which is more fact-based vs opinion-based. Then there's the facts, which are usually somewhere in between. Subjectively, I was disruptive to the class. Objectively, I was a little too talkative. The facts are that I loved to speak, socialize, and connect with my fellow classmates and maybe the teacher could have employed a more effective method for curbing my behavior.

Let's face it – there are better alternatives than shaming a child by having them walk around school with a degrading label on their back. As a 7-year-old, those moments were the foundation of some of the mental blocks I had in my young adult life. They prohibited the growth of the rich reality mindset that brews in every young mind while it's open to life's many possibilities. I'm referring to those thoughts, dreams, and lives we envision for ourselves based on the innate rights we know we have been given by our Creator. These experiences put limitations on my freethinking 7-year-old mind, to the point that I became quieter and quieter with every grade advancement. I became less talkative, more serious, and more hesitant to "disrupt the class" A dull version of my once vibrant self.

REFLECTIVE QUESTIONS:

Can you think of some ways others may have dulled your shine?

What were some of the things that they said to you?

You believed them then, but what is your perspective now? What are the facts?

_____

_____

_____

_____

_____

_____

_____

_____

_____

_____

_____

CHAPTER TWO

LIMITS ON A RICH MIND

SECOND GRADE FOUND me in Mrs. Quinn's class at Monte Vista Elementary. Here, talking was much more embraced. Not during lectures, of course, but more so during what Mrs. Quinn liked to call "show and tell." It was always when we were fresh off the weekend with lots to tell our school friends. We had the chance to stand up and share with the class what our weekend was like. These were the moments I lived for – because we all know I'm a social butterfly and I find pleasure in connecting and talking with others (not that I really understood this as a child, but that was because no one embraced my social skills). When it was my turn to tell the class what my weekend was like and the teacher called my name, I would, without hesitation, go straight to the front of the class and share my weekend adventures. It felt like most of us had the same energy and passion for sharing during Show and Tell and for socializing with our fellow classmates. As youths, I think we all tend to share the commonality of being vibrant and fearless – especially when encouraged by our caregivers. I wasn't quite dull and quiet just yet. The suppression of my passion and vibrancy had only started a year prior, so when Ms. Quinn would ask our class questions, I still had a little bit of that chatty spirit. Even still, my experience with Mrs. Quinn presented its own challenges on my rich reality journey. Let's keep going.

I've always had this 'fetish' for zoning out and touching my juicy, baby-skin-soft left ear when I'm deep in thought or closely observing something. I remember touching my ear and Ms. Quinn mocking me by literally copying exactly what I was doing in an attempt to make fun of and correct my body language behavior. Now let's remember, I was 8 years old, in the second grade, and completely unaware of the importance of body language. I remember her making a clown face at me, sticking her tongue out or opening her mouth wide, and expanding her ears the way monkeys do. This was her way of making me feel like I was doing something wrong. And, well, it too was a negative interference on my road to my rich reality. In retrospect, it felt like another attempt to take away my freedom of expression. I wonder, did my first and second grade teachers have discussions on what to expect from different students upon that student's arrival into their class? Could this be a subjective student record following me from one grade to the next? Maybe. Maybe not. All I know is it didn't feel good. During these couple of years of my educational experience with two teachers, I was questioning how I talked, how I walked, and how I thought – and I was only 8 years old and in the second grade. I was already developing insecurities within myself because of the adults my parents had entrusted to care for me for eight hours every day.

These were all examples of the limits imposed on a rich mind full of boundless ideas and possibilities. At home, my rich mind could imagine the idea of flying unicorns, tooth fairy visitations leaving money under my pillow, and Santa Claus bringing me gifts because I had been a good boy. But at school there was a contradiction. At home I felt empowered to think whatever I wanted about myself or the world, to be myself; during school I must talk, walk, and act a way that didn't match my true character. It was confusing. Instead of figuring out ways to create a rich reality for ourselves so we can go off into the world as adults and contribute to a society that embraces that rich reality, which some call the American Dream, we're too busy unraveling all the social constructs that have been placed on us since we started talking. Follow the guidelines or risk being ridiculed and reprimanded. The problem with the guidelines is that they hinder the development of creating a rich reality for yourself. I know you can relate to these thoughts and feelings. Let's continue.

During fifth grade we were given a green card/red card system. In simple terms, you would start off with a green card and, if you were nearly perfect all day long – e.g., not whispering to your classmates during class – you would keep the green card. I often wondered if the teachers used these cards liberally or sparingly. At this point, I was 11 years of age. A bit older and a bit more constructed by someone else's guidelines. I was a bit more conditioned to think, talk, and walk the way my teachers wanted me to, but I was also a bit more over it and less patient. It became harder for me to change my personality at the drop of a dime between home and school and I was giving up all hope that my teachers would ever understand me. I came to the conclusion that this was something I would just have to deal with for 8 miserable hours per day until I was no longer required to go to school. The only thing I loved about school at that age was sports, talking to my friends, and lunchtime. My reputation in school for being a disruptive, talkative, misunderstood boy that loved touching his soft, pillowy ears followed and preceded me. It was such common knowledge that when it was time to choose students to be the teacher's helper, the school speaker, or for other extracurricular activities, I was usually overlooked. I resented that and my behavior started to present itself as rebellion.

I started to wonder – does this type of stuff happen with adults? Do adults walk around telling other adults "you can't whisper quietly during a lecture"? Should children be subjected to these types of guidelines during those precious, open-minded years of discovery? I respectfully and humbly say no. And, just to be clear, I'm not speaking of the kids jumping on tables and running around the classroom uncontrollably like they're at a birthday party. I'm speaking of the kids, adults, and people that were most likely living within their natural element at that age and simply being their vibrant selves. If life has taught me anything, it's the importance of living in your natural element. This is one of the essential and most important tools for turning your dreams into your rich reality. Alongside living in your natural element, there are many tools that can be used while on your journey to creating your rich reality. The other essential elements are having an open mind, trusting your own thoughts, and being comfortable with your perception of yourself. Because, at the end of the day, only you know yourself better than anyone else. It all starts with you, within your own mind.

REFLECTIVE QUESTIONS:

On a scale of 1 to 10, with 10 being 100%, to what extent are you living in your natural element?

What are some ways you can live more in your natural element?

What could living more in your natural element do for your mindset and for your life? What would it empower you to do? Who would it empower you to be?

_____

_____

_____

_____

_____

_____

_____

_____

_____

CHAPTER THREE

THREE SIDES TO EVERY STORY

SO FAR, WE'VE heard about two perspectives of the things that placed limits on my rich mind and thereby contributed to me losing my rich reality – my side and my teachers' side. Now let's broaden the perspective even further and talk just a little about the third side. The perspective of the parents... the lovely first teachers.

One of the ways to prevent some of these experiences I had as a child and to ensure your child's dreams become a rich reality is to ask your child questions.

I think, as parents, guardians, tios, aunts, abuelos, grandmas, ummas, appas, nani's, bibi's etc., it's important to ask the children in your life questions on a regular basis, like:

- Do you like your teacher?
- Do you like what you're being taught?
- What do you want to be when you grow up?
- What are some of your favorite things to do?

It's a fact that our tax dollars go towards covering the school's operation costs and we should make sure our youth are happy with what they're learning. They are our only hope for solving some of the social issues that exist in America as we speak. I mean, the way Americans communicate with each other on a national and global level isn't the best, at least from my experiences. We don't do a good enough job of telling each other how we truly feel. We bottle it up, hide it in the closet, and keep it deeply embedded in our thoughts, never sharing it with anyone until we reach our boiling point. My boiling point was feeling like I was living a poor reality.

Too often we forget that young humans have thoughts of their own and shouldn't just be treated as young, undeveloped minds. Rather, they should actually be treated like the minds of stakeholders in the continued evolution of this universe. They're minds that interpret, learn, perceive, rationalize, comprehend, and develop.

The fact I so vividly remember the stifling reactions of my rich mind proves the notion that our minds are highly impressionable and constantly taking in our experiences, starting all the way back from the ages of three or four. Some would argue it actually begins in the womb. Studies have shown that when a mother-to-be speaks to or rubs her belly, the baby sometimes starts off by kicking and causing war within the mother's womb. However, when she practices deep breathing exercises, reads, or plays soft music, the baby will calm down. What I find highly interesting, though, is that while we might not even consciously remember those moments, maybe we do remember subconsciously.

Going into more depth about being a 3-year-old and feeling like you can take on the whole world alone, our parents come in to sort of check and balance that limitless thinking. I feel like I had a positive system of checks and balances in the form of my parents. They didn't push any limiting programming on me – they only expected me to be a kid, respectfully. Their allowing me to figure things out as I went along helped me maintain parts of my rich reality and continue to pursue the possibilities it entailed. It is important for parents to allow those freedoms of expression so that they do not suppress a child's limitless, rich mindset. As our first teachers, parents have the advantage of instilling in a child's mind the idea that "you can do anything you put your mind to." What's unfortunate, though, is that parents can sometimes forget the things they taught you when you were seven and then switch it up on you as you get older, as they start telling you to be practical and to conform to societal standards. It's then that we find that they've checked off more than what's required and kept us from propelling into our rich reality.

Then when you start to move towards your adolescent years, like 7 to 15, our teachers become our mentors. It's like our parents place our mental maturity in the hands of other adults who aren't even living their own rich reality. No wonder so many people get caught up in the rat race and lose their way on their journey to their bliss!

Now don't get me wrong, I think it's safe to say that people don't set out in their life to be the reason someone else's life doesn't prosper, or the cause for someone else's mental limitations and/or insecurities. Most times it happens organically. As humans, we have a tendency to project and deflect a lot of our internal thoughts onto others (I've been guilty of this, too). For example, have you ever heard someone tell you they're having a weird craving for something like pickles with Kool-Aid? While that used to be one of my favorite snacks, I'm sure the average person would agree it's a pretty unique food combination to crave. Well, if I were to express my desire to enjoy some pickles with Kool-Aid, I might receive reactions like, "That's disgusting! Why would you eat that?" or "That's super unhealthy! Why would someone inflict that much damage on their bodies?" This is an example of deflecting our own views and internal thoughts onto someone else. All taste buds are not created equally! In the same way, all minds are not created equally either. We must become more aware of the evident truth that we are mentally wired to perceive and interpret things differently. It isn't uncommon to be on the same page as someone and yet see something slightly or completely different – hence, the reason there are different religions, political parties, clubs, sports, foods, states, cities, countries, etc. Those were all born of people that had different perspectives on one topic.

REFLECTIVE QUESTIONS:

Think back to your childhood. How would you describe your parents' effect on your freethinking rich mind?

What are some thought patterns you were taught that may have put limits on your rich mind?

What do you now know or feel to be the truth of those thought patterns?

_____

_____

_____

_____

_____

_____

_____

_____

_____

CHAPTER FOUR

SELF SABOTAGING THE RICH MIND

AS I SWITCH gears and explain a couple more things that personally held me back from my deserved rich reality, I must say this: no one is responsible for anyone else's rich reality. This reality can only come from the individual on their individual journey, which is you! It's called personal responsibility. Sometimes, we're our own worst enemies by what we allow to influence our minds and rich reality. Let's discuss some of the ways in which we can sabotage our own rich minds – three self-imposed obstacles you may face on your journey to turning your dreams into a rich reality.

PROCRASTINATION

Procrastination is the first obstacle to

making anything become a reality. And, boy, did I procrastinate! I procrastinated in life. I procrastinated writing this book! When re-activating my gym membership, starting a new career, and the list goes on. The key is to never let that be your obstacle. Procrastination isn't always intentional or noticeable. Sometimes, the things of everyday life – like jobs, kids, and drama – can cause us to procrastinate. Herein lies the importance of intention. When something is done intentionally, you are more aware of your actions... and the consequences sometimes, too. When something is done unintentionally, you may not be aware of your actions or the effect it is having on your rich reality life.

UNINTENTIONALITY

I wasn't always aware of people's intentions when choosing my friendships. My grandma would always say "birds of a feather flock together," which means we go in similar directions as our peers. Sometimes these are good directions; sometimes they're bad. This is the unintentionality I'm talking about. Spending time with friends, overlooking their patterns, behaviors, and mindsets, and ultimately overlooking how these are affecting our lives.

I chose bad friends throughout school. I'm not really talking about the first grade to the fifth grade, because for the most part everyone was still innocent. Well, not me. I was a disruptor and a lover of my chunky, juicy right ear lobe, but I digress. I'm speaking more of my junior high years. These were the friends of greatest influence. The kids that liked to ditch school or used a lot of expletives. These experiences inevitably slowed down my journey to a rich reality. Once I paid attention to the substance of my conversations with these so-called friends and the type of person I was during these friendships, my momentum began to increase a bit. There was the potential of a rich reality awaiting me. This was the first step in the right direction to free my mind of a poor reality. We must choose our friends wisely. Friends are an integral part of a person's mental journey and discovery of their rich reality. Friends can work with your interests or against them. Our friends should share similar ideas. Not like political ideas or food ideas but more mindsets – their ways of thinking. Their perspectives. And we have to be intentional not just in choosing friends but in every aspect of our lives.

LACK OF OBSERVATION

Some would agree, therefore, that the United States constitution was created for this very same theory: that we are all entitled to a rich reality. In my experience, my rich reality was stalled by not understanding my own reality because I wasn't doing enough soul searching or observation of what was going on around me.

All along, even as a first and second grader, my teachers also had the same examples we have today. As adults, they should have done a better job at being examples of those very same principles they claimed to follow and uphold as great citizens of the United States of America. I leave it to you to think about this – maybe you can let me know those thoughts and enlighten me. America, on its face, promotes a rich reality. This country is what inspired my rich reality: without the examples around me, I never would have known what I was seeking. My examples consist of friends, movies, parents, TV shows, experiences, etcetera. GOOD examples are tools that will help you achieve a rich reality. Observation can be one very good tool to employ.

REFLECTIVE QUESTIONS:

Are you choosing your path with intention? Your friends, your actions, etc.?

Consider the people you have around you on a regular basis. Are they limited thinkers? Do they give good advice?

Are you observing your surroundings with open eyes and an open heart? Take a moment and do so now. Do you have good examples around you? What about what you watch on TV or the internet? What do you listen to regularly?

_____

_____

_____

_____

_____

_____

_____

PART TWO

FINDING YOUR RICH REALITY

CHAPTER FIVE

THE AWAKENING

AFTER THE OBSTACLES comes the momentum of change. This is when you first realize you have been robbed of dreaming rich and it's time to change your reality. Every person, species, and universe has the right to dream rich. We have the right to think what we want to think about ourselves and we have the right to dream big. We have the right to dream all day about who we want to become, then take massive actions to make those dreams a reality.

It's easy to fall into the pattern of procrastinating by dreaming 80% of the time with no follow-up, leaving you with only 20% of your time to turn your dreams into a rich reality. That's why it took me years to set the time aside to share my thoughts on this topic.

It took me years to come up with the name for this book. It took me years to turn my dreams into a rich reality, so I could finally live the rich experience that I've always deserved and that every human on earth deserves. Manifesting your rich reality can truly be a lifelong journey, but it all starts the same: with an awakening.

Between the ages of 16 and 18, I found myself coming of age in a pretty non-diverse city. And, as a result, I began to experience stereotypical, biased, racial profiling and judgment which started to make me second-guess my own identity. This lowered my self-esteem, confidence, and ambition, causing me to make multiple career changes throughout my journey of self-discovery. I would over-analyze my actions and try to figure out what I was doing wrong. Of course, I now realize I wasn't doing anything wrong. I was just being me. So, if you're in a place in your life where you're feeling a lack of drive or are low in confidence and questioning yourself and your actions, then you, my friend, may be on the verge of awakening to your rich reality journey. You are on your way to releasing the doubt and anxiety that are part of the poor reality you've been living.

This is exciting. This is a time to revisit the moments in your life when you can remember having a rich mind and living in a rich reality – even if you have to think back as far as seven years old! It will help you get in touch with the rich feelings and perspectives associated with those times so you can tap back into them. This will help you to cure your rich mind amnesia and remember who you are. Once you begin to become more aware of your limitless self, you become free (and should then begin) to do things that light you up! In the next chapter we'll discuss practical ways you can begin to take actionable steps towards your rich reality today.

REFLECTIVE QUESTIONS:

Do you feel you're in an awakening right now? What does it look and feel like?

Are you excited to be in this place of transition?

Think back to a time when you were limitless and fearless. Close your eyes and place yourself back in that scenario. What did that look and feel like?

_____

_____

_____

_____

_____

_____

_____

_____

_____

_____

CHAPTER SIX

THE PATHWAY

THE PATHWAY BACK to your rich reality is a marathon, not a sprint. It's a daily grind in which you continually sharpen your ability to do. It's not the flip of a switch but a momentum that starts with that one thought of "I love myself! I love who I am and the way I do things." This translates into more intentional actions, more productivity, and doing things that you love doing. It's the little things like going after and getting that job you've always wanted, making a monthly date to take yourself to the movies, exercising and eating healthily to obtain your wellness goals, or going to the lake for a weekend to spend quality time with people you care about.

Initially, I had no limitations for any poor realities. When I talk about limits, I'm referring to mindset limits. For example, happiness is a rich reality and sadness is a poor reality. As I've already explained, as kids we have examples like teachers, parents, and sometimes mentors that teach us about limitations. There is an unintentional fear that is stoked in our minds and souls early on: sometimes it's subtle, sometimes and for some it's blatant. Sometimes it's in the name of love. Sometimes it's not. You don't have to remain in a poor state of mind.

To truly unlock your rich dreams and make them a reality, you must figure out your course of action to becoming an unlimited thinker. We must also individually find our own personal paths to reach a rich mindset and turn that into a rich reality. There are no wrong or right ways to activate your rich mindset and trying beats failure every time. Let's explore the details of the pathway to a rich reality. The following are some tools you can utilize to step into your unlimited, rich state of mind.

VISUALIZATION

Where does your rich reality take place? This is not limited to one place, it's wherever you want to live out your life of bliss. It could be at the beach, at the movies, at the dog park, at a friend's house, at a basketball game, or maybe even at your daughter's dance recital. Where are the places you want to frequent because they bring out the rich mind and feelings in you? Spend more time in these places. Yes, it really is that simple. A rich reality has no boundaries. It could even be life with your significant other.

What will you do in the places of your rich reality? How will you choose to think – limited or limitless? What will you set your intentions to learn? It is in this place where you flex your observation muscles in ways that work for your well-being. Maybe read more books and listen to more podcasts that fuel the journey you're on. We'll talk more on this later, but what I want you to get is that you can determine what your reality looks and feels like. How? By forming good habits, picking the right mentors, experiences, perceptions, and friendships, and understanding that they all shape our thoughts and perceptions. Then you will be making strides on the pathway to your rich reality. Why is this important? Well, that's simple: because it feels damn good to live a rich reality life without any limitations in your thoughts, actions, and experiences. Because this is the reason why you are here – to have an abundant life!

INTENTIONAL INFLUENCE

Have you ever heard the phrase, "time is money"? Well, here's an unpopular opinion: time is not money because money comes and goes. Time is eternal. Time is more like gold because it is rare yet can last forever. We must choose wisely when we decide who we share our time with. Why?

We never intend to catch a cold but, if we're exposed to it, sometimes we'll catch one. As children, we innocently think we can do any and everything. That is, until life teaches us how to balance and color within the lines. To avoid the far right or the far left and play it safe in the middle. We were big dreamers! Until our influencers – that is, the people we hung around – started to instill fear and limitations into our minds. Now, in all fairness, sometimes the fear is justified. However, fear, self-doubt, self-pity, and low self-esteem are all mental roadblocks to turning our dreams into a rich reality. If we're not careful, our influencers can lead us towards a limited mind, thus adding to the obstacles in the way of making our dreams into a rich reality. Think of your mind like an immune system. You must build it up and strengthen it; you must exercise and protect it.

A great start to strengthening the mind is to choose the right mentors, friends, and relationships. The key here is to be intentional and to choose them by their mindsets. The old saying goes "judge a man or a woman by the fruits of their labor." Well, the fruits of their labor are a result of their mindsets, their energy, their advice, etc., not their material wealth. What is the right mentor? Good question. Stay questioning, my friends ;).

I define a mentor as someone that hears and understands you when you speak. You can relate to them and, when they speak, it penetrates the fabric of your life and soul. The right mentor gives insight and new perspectives that can be applied to your dreams becoming a rich reality. I have been blessed to be mentored by some amazing authors, millionaires, billionaires, college professors, politicians, and more.

To take it a step further, don't be afraid to learn from people you don't fully agree with or those that doesn't share your visions, ideas, or beliefs. They can still show you or teach you ways to manifest your dreams. Sometimes they could be an example of what you don't want to become or a source for effective life lessons on making your dream a rich reality faster!

Once you're aware that everything that goes into your mind is just as important as everything that goes into your body, you will be much more selective as to what you choose to let in. To have a robust mind is to have a robust immune system. For example, if a car receives the wrong type of oil, the car will become aware and warn the driver of the possible outcomes. If the driver doesn't take heed, this could damage the car. Likewise, if you're not taking responsibility for what you allow into your mind, then you could destroy your chances of living a rich reality. Constantly taking in bad advice? Then prepare to continue to make bad decisions. Energy is contagious:

Every word spoken to you or over you is a new seed planted to grow in your mind. If it's a good seed, it will turn into a rich experience which would be a rich reality. If it's a bad seed, it will grow into insecurity, self-doubt, anger, anxiety, and so on.

So how can we uproot the bad seeds that have been planted by influencers up until now? I thought long and hard on what life I wanted for myself and how I saw myself vs what another person saw for me. Then I started with replacing the music I listened to, choosing more empowering TV shows, and removing bad friendships that weren't feeding my soul. Believe it or not, those are the major influences in most of our lives that have an impact on our reality. Once I removed my influences, I started to discover new influences. And the replanting began. I listened to, watched, and spent time around things and people that reflected the life I knew I wanted to live. I wanted to become a Media Proprietor -- someone that creates, directs, and organizes media in a way that engages people. In my position, you must be multi-faceted and always open-minded to new ideas, concepts, and cultures in order to create media that is relatable. So, I started to watch more TED Talks, read self-help books, and listen to motivational speakers. It soon became a habit. It became my new program.

That's the beauty of free choice: we are all entitled to choose the program. Choose the program of our rich reality.

SEE THE ABUNDANCE

The world around us is so unlimited that we still haven't even discovered everything that lies in the depths of the oceans! So why do we set limits on our potential? The universe is overflowing with abundance: we therefore truly have no limits in terms of who we can be and what we can become. Let's look at the world, for example – you have millions if not billions of plants, species, complexions, grains of sand, food styles, dances, and religions. These are all hints and non-verbal cues to never set limitations on your mind. The world is abundant, no matter how many people try to make you believe that the world is full of limits. The thing is, when people share their experiences and/or views on the world, it is exactly that: "their view." That is why it's important for us to be aware of our own views. You must be able to identify your own version of a rich reality.

BEING PRESENT

We've all got one shot at life and an unknown number of new days, each 24 hours long, to manifest our rich reality. You only turn 18, 21, or 25 once and it's pointless to live as if you're still in that year. Why? Because you're in this present time, with a new opportunity to manifest your rich reality. Being in the present moment has a humongous impact on the mindset. If you're constantly looking forward or backward, you are distracted from the now.

This happened to me many times – there are similarities to procrastination, but it's the unintentional procrastination I speak of. I was just following the program that I chose for myself. It was merely habitual and comfortable to me: it felt right at the time and it was a part of my soul and my reality. I was getting caught up in this daily dose of someone else's reality.

There's nothing wrong with occasionally reminiscing on good times or reliving good moments in your mind. However, don't let it distract you from creating new and maybe even better moments now. You stop your growth and limit your mind when you do this.

Take a moment and reflect on this. We're made up of everything within the universe. Like us, the ants have a function, a mind, and a purpose. The water in the ocean is like the continuous saliva forming in our mouths. The rain is like our tears, replenishing us and releasing the swelled-up clouds of water within us. The sun and the core of the earth are heat, like the 98.7 Fahrenheit our bodies are set at. The wind is like the breath we breathe as it flows in and out with every inhale and exhale. What's the point? The point is: the earth moves forward every single day. Like clockwork and without hiccups, the sun rises and the seasons change to spring, summer, fall, and winter. The universe continues to progress. The universe is always striving for the best and working towards a rich reality. In fact, the universe already is a rich reality – we have been tasked with elevating ourselves to its level of richness. These perceptions I share with you are meant to be new seeds planted within your mental garden, to grow and manifest into your very own rich reality.

ACTIVITY:

WRITE THE VISION: What does your rich reality look like? Feel like? Where are you? Who's there with you? What are you doing? Can you see the abundance? What is it made of? How are you making sure you remain present in the moment?

_____

_____

_____

_____

_____

_____

_____

_____

_____

_____

_____

CONCLUSION

YOUR JOURNEY IS JUST BEGINNING

THESE ARE JUST a few habits I've noticed and I think are good to have when finding your rich reality. Some of these tools and learned habits help you align with everything around you in a way where you will no longer inflect your ideas onto others. Rather, you will respect others in a way that is beneficial to peace and prosperity. With the right tools and once you've observed your mental limitations, you can choose your approach on how to push past the limitations. What we do with what we see, hear, learn, and feel can be used for us or against us. The choice is literally up to you.

After reading this book, something like a light may turn on within you. I may spark something inside of you that had been waiting for years to come out or I may give you the direction you need in setting your mindset. I can't tell you how to think. However, what I can share is the tools I used that helped me make my dreams my very own rich reality. I hope this book was insightful and beneficial to you. Always focus on the best version of yourself and fight hard to get back to the default stage of just being.

The best advice I – or anyone – could give a young person is to always dream rich. Believe in your ability to create the version of your own rich reality, which could look like a painter, a business owner, a hair stylist, or an optician... Anything!

ABOUT THE AUTHOR

AMIR SHAHEED

WHEN YOU HEAR about Amir Shaheed, the first thing that may come to mind is creativity at it's best and his passion, determination, and brilliant intuition when it comes to providing consumers across the globe with original and engaging content. He is a Media Proprietor who conceptualizes and funds TV shows, movies, and exclusive content.

Amir Shaheed's success in his craft can be credited to his vast knowledge of the industry and career trajectory. His love for sparking something within people stems from the motivation he gets from prominent media personalities and major headliners like Mark Burnett, Oprah Winfrey, Pharrell, and Tyler Perry. A pioneer in the business of coordinating media activities, he projects a high level of technical competence, self-confidence, authority, and enthusiasm in doing what he loves to do best.

Amir Shaheed started his training as an A&R with UMG and WME. His media approach is informed by his years of experience orchestrating results amid the fast-paced environment and by choosing to work with the right people. A master of his craft, he constantly researches the inner workings of the entertainment industry and harnesses his ideas and creativity to turn what he envisions into actual art. As a hard worker and creative thinker, Amir Shaheed devotes all his time, energy, and passion to ensuring that his TV shows, movies, and content gets the best attention it deserves.

He is sought after by both individuals and organizations for his creative prowess. Ornamented with a dynamic personality, Amir Shaheed prefers to take the extra steps in staying unique and reaching his aspirations.

Putting exceptional content out there in the form of clients, shows, books and more is the driving force behind everything he does.

www.ingramcontent.com/pod-product-compliance
Lightning Source LLC
Chambersburg PA
CBHW070102100426
42743CB00012B/2641